Black Marigolds
and
Coloured Stars

E. POWYS MATHERS.

E. POWYS MATHERS

Black Marigolds

AND

Coloured Stars

WITH AN INTRODUCTION BY
TONY HARRISON

ANVIL PRESS POETRY

Published in 2004
by Anvil Press Poetry Ltd
Neptune House 70 Royal Hill London SE10 8RF
www.anvilpresspoetry.com

This book is published
with financial assistance from
Arts Council England

A catalogue record for this book
is available from the British Library

Coloured Stars and *Black Marigolds* were first published
in 1919 by B. H. Blackwell, Oxford
The frontispiece portrait is by Hester Sainsbury
from *Eastern Love*, vols. I and II, London, 1927

Designed and set in Monotype Dante by Anvil
Printed at Alden Press Limited
Oxford and Northampton

NOTE ON THE TEXT

This edition follows the texts of the 1919 editions without
alteration, except for the change from italic to roman of
"Give me your" in the last line of stanza 27 of *Black Marigolds*.
These texts were reprinted without change in *Love Songs
of Asia* (Pushkin Press, London, 1944).

Contents

Black Marigolds

Even Now

IT'S ALMOST fifty years since I came across *Black Marigolds*. From a much-frequented stall in Leeds Market, I picked up, for a pound, the wonderful *Anthology of World Poetry* edited by Mark Van Doren (1929). Even now I always buy copies if I see them to give to others. Its over 1,200 pages include translations of poems from Chinese, Japanese, Sanskrit, Arabic, Persian, Hebrew, Egyptian, Greek, Latin, Italian, Spanish, French, German, Scandinavian, Russian, as well as English, Irish, American poems.

Among all these mostly unknown foreign treasures one discovery began to haunt me from the moment I first read it in the 50's: *Black Marigolds*, a version of the Sanskrit *Chaurapanchasika* by Edward Powys Mathers. It seemed somewhere to chime with remembered complex childhood feelings of the pleasure of, say, biting into a beautiful apple in our bomb-shelter cellar as German bombers droned above; and then in the 50's with the teenage apprehension of individual death at the same time as the unfathomable well of sensuality. The epigraph attributed to Azeddin El Mocadecci, which I am now inclined to believe is a brilliant invention of Mathers, stayed so vividly in my mind for forty years that when I was making a film about three women with Alzheimer's and noticed that the floor on the psychiatric hospital was decorated with mosaics of black daisies and that all the women had photographs of their by now forgotten weddings beside their hospital beds, I called the film *Black Daisies for the Bride*. It was directly inspired by Mathers' epigraph to *Black Marigolds*: "And sometimes we look to the end of the tale that there should be marriage-feasts, and find

7

only, as it were, black marigolds and a silence." I was looking for a way to dramatise a mode of affirmation in women whose capacity for recall was gone, and who were prisoners of oblivion. The *Even now* of *Black Marigolds* became my talisman, for the dark affirmation in that film, and in my life.

Whenever I came across any book with the name of Edward Powys Mathers on the spine I bought it and now have a good many, including a first edition of *Black Marigolds* (1919), though as they were mostly the sort of mildly erotic Eastern literature published "for subscribers" or from publishers of fine books like the Golden Cockerel Press they have never been easy to come by, and too expensive when they could be found. I wanted to know more about the poet-translator but there were only the most tantalising clues, which seem appropriate enough for Edward Powys Mathers who, as well as being a translator of Eastern poetry, had more fame and repute as Torquemada the setter of crossword puzzles for the *Observer*. Torquemada is even now setting us puzzles. Some of his crosswords have clues which make up a poem that rhymes from clue to clue and many of his "original" poems are hidden behind cyphers. The autobiographical clues are as hard to solve as Torquemada's. But his wife Rosamond in a memoir prefaced to a collection of his best crossword puzzles gives us a few facts.

Edward Powys Mathers was born at Forest Hill on 26th August 1892 and died 3rd February 1939. He was at Trinity College, Oxford from 1910 to the outbreak of the First World War. Although everyone remembers him as suffering from unspecified "illness" he had himself finally accepted as a private in the 24th Middlesex Regiment, though he was after some months given his discharge. He seems, characteristically, to have been extremely quick and efficient at decoding cyphers which earned the budding Torquemada, generally known to close friends as "Bill", the nickname of "Willy the Cypher King". At one of the camps where he was billeted as assistant to the Medical Officer (either Woldingham, Halton or Northampton), Cecil French, a fellow private with literary tastes, remembers that "*Black Marigolds* his first translation was in progress". And Mathers himself tell us that "my rendering was finished in 1915, in two or three sessions on a box by the stove in hutments". Since Mathers admits to having only "a very small smattering of Sanskrit" and, indeed, that all his Eastern poetry was "translated at second-hand", he probably had to make use of a previous translation of the *Chaurapanchasika* by Sir Edwin Arnold who did know Sanskrit and published in 1896 the Sanskrit text and his verse rendition in his own handwriting with his watercolours of tropical flowers and Indian scenes. Mathers points out almost in the same words as Arnold that each stanza in the original starts with *adyapi*, "a word of reminiscence". Arnold writes that this repeated Sanskrit word gives to the stanzas "a melodious and ingenious monotony of fanciful passion" and Mathers that it gives to the poem "a recurring monotone of retrospection, which I hope my unchanging *Even now* also suggests." Arnold varies his response to the recurrent word as in "I die, but I remember!"; "Dying I recall"; "I die, yet well I mind ..."; "Ah, dying – dying – I remember"; "Yet I will die remembering" and then finally in stanza 27 comes up with the phrase that Mathers lifted to make the heart of the captive condemned lover affirm his celebration in the shadow of death:

And, even now, when any dawn may bring
Such as shall slay me to the prison-gate ...

It is also possible that he lifted the phrase "Even now" from Arthur A. Macdonell's *A History of Sanskrit Literature* (1900) which speaks of the 50 stanzas of the *Chaurapanchasika* "each beginning with the phrase 'Even now I remember'."

Whatever the source E. P. M. had the dramatic instinct to use the repeated "Even now" with the effect of both passing bell and the beat of the condemned but affirmative and death-defying heart. In the pause before each second line comes in we hear the bell toll which opens the condemned captive's mind and heart to his sensual memories. They remain in the celebratory kaleidoscope in his soul until the last brilliant line which is pure Mathers:

> The heavy knife. As to a gala day.

The darkness and the colours make each other more profound. All the *Even now*s tolling with certain mortality nonetheless fill the heart so full of sensual recall that it goes out to execution with the gaiety of a gala.

The phrase *Even now* reverberates beyond the poem to the time and place of its translation, affirming the sensual at the time of the 1914–18 war in the hutments of an army camp where we know Mathers composed it. *Even now* asserts the sensual fullness of all the translations in this book which were done in the same period. Even now in times of darkness and extinction the passions of the heart and the pleasures of the sensual body have to be remembered. Even now the child slowly relishes his apple with unfriendly Fokkers growling overhead. In a time of war the idea of death tomorrow for a young man of 23 as Mathers was would have been extremely common, though not for the offence of loving a Kashmiri princess. Bearing in mind that they were written in World War One they have something of the sensual tonic of the silk-clad odalisques of Matisse in World War Two, and of my childhood apple!

Charles Tomlinson in his *Oxford Book of Verse in English Translation*, which surprisingly does not include Mathers, claims that Ezra Pound's *Cathay* with its Chinese poems of parting or frontier service had an implicit link to the campaigns in France of World War One and quotes Hugh Kenner as saying "*Cathay* is largely a war-book". One can say something similar about *Black Marigolds* in which Mathers' *Even now* allows us to hear the passing bells of World War One tolling behind a passionate sensual recall. But to achieve that celebratory note it has to have an exotic location. It couldn't come from the Front even though men under the shadow of death dreamed of their women at home. The darkness of the same shadow enhances the delicate sensualities of *Coloured Stars*, published in the same year as *Black Marigolds*, 1919. The title is taken from a line in "Song" (p. 39):

> If our clear blue night full of white stars
> Turned to a night of coloured stars . . .

This poem along with "English Girl" (p. 50), the one poem by which Mathers is represented in W. B. Yeats' *Oxford Book of Modern Verse*, and "Being Together at Night" (p. 44) is attributed by Mathers in his note to an American-born Chinese, a valet by profession. He names him as J. Wing (1870–1923) – "or Julius Wing as he hated to be called!". E. Allen Ashwin in a memoir prefixed to a collection of Torquemada's puzzles says that J. Wing and John Duncan, the "lowland Scot" responsible for the Arabic poem "Climbing Up to You" (p. 57), "represent one of their author's most successful flights in imaginative fiction." They are both without a doubt among E. P. M.'s Pessoan *personae*.

He gives much longer sequences to both in later books and much more elaborate and suspicious biography. J. Wing's "The Green Paper Lanterns" appears in Volume XI of *The Eastern Anthology* and Mathers elaborates on his life: "He might have inherited a great charcuterie business" but he became "a sort of chasseur at hotels in San Francisco and Saint Louis, and a gentleman's gentleman in New York and Boston. Later he shook cocktails, and contributed verse in English to three or four American journals. As a valet he visited England, France, Spain and Italy. He perished of consumption in lodgings by the harbour at Vigo in 1925, just as the boat on which I had come to visit him was mooring under a green dawn cloudy with gulls." He claims to have spent six months in the island of Tenerife with Wing in 1921. It is interesting to note that they were, supposedly, in Oratava, the place where Sir Edwin Arnold wrote his version of the *Chaurapanchasika*. Torquemada clues?

He tells us that in the poems of J. Wing "opium and wine speak for themselves". It seems that Mathers used both the translations of genuine poems from Eastern poets and those from the invented *personae* as a safer context for what are hinted at in the meagre reminiscences as alcoholism and drug addiction and bisexuality which Mathers needed to place in an exotic Eastern location to address. He certainly found the sexual reticence of the English poetic tradition frustrating, and he praises the Islamic poet who "takes his veneration and description from the navel to the knee without altering his key of worship. Few English poets have been able to do this." He complains in an essay on Arabic prose and verse that "from Chaucer to the great Victorians, poets could not mention the female pudenda without waiting, as it were, for the laugh to follow. Breasts they could manage and remain the devout lover; but the rest was a matter for mirth."

Christopher Sandford, who took over the Golden Cockerel Press from Robert Gibbings in 1933, described E. P. M. in a 1980 letter to Michael Dawson, another would-be solver of the puzzle of Mathers, as an "alcoholic", "bearded, wide and squat" but adds that he was the most benevolent man he'd ever met, though he implies that the beaming benevolence owed much to the amount he'd imbibed and the level of his inebriation. He also said that E. P. M. was "very loving – maybe too loving – with women and men" and describes how Mathers made a dead set at seducing him.

Just as in the invented poems of the Chinese-American Julius Wing "opium and wine speak for themselves", so in his short scenarios, what he calls "the squibs" of *Red Wise*, on the life of the real Abu Nowas with invented incidents and poems, there is much wine drinking and a chapter on experiments with chewing *bhang* that only a genuine devotee could imagine. There is one poem attributed to Abu Nowas in which the beauty of the whole world turns into wine and becomes quaffable:

> If He made all beauty out of wine
> He'd get no worship to compare with mine:
> For, when my purse were flat and credit far,
> I'd suck the golden nipple of a star
> Or that blue grape He dangles up on high,
> The infinite first vintage of the sky . . .

He further elaborates on John Duncan (1877–1919), the supposed author of "Climbing Up to You" (p. 57), in the next book he published, *The Garden of Bright Waters: One Hundred and Twenty Asiatic Love Poems* (Oxford, 1920). He makes him a lowland Scot who lived in Edinburgh until he was between 20 and 25, and, after a disastrous love affair, left Scotland and in two years was an established member of a small tribe of nomadic Arabs, travelling up and down with them the whole line of the south-west coast of the Persian Gulf. He married an Arab and all his forty-odd poems are addressed to her. Like this one, "Sand", with another metamorphosis of the world into first milk, then the always welcome wine!

> The sand is like acres of wet milk
> Poured out under the moonlight;
> It crawls up about your brown feet
> Like wine trodden from white stars.

Once alerted to the pseudonymous *personae* you begin to suspect them everywhere. In the 12 volumes of *The Eastern Anthology* E. P. M. claims as one of the real "discoveries" of the whole series which covers Cambodian, Japanese, Arabic, Bengali, Sanskrit, Chinese, Turkish poetry and stories, all translated from the French, a poem called "A Love Song" where "there is a reaction under wine and a letting go ... [where] the poet swings back to the old severe intricacies of versification and, with them, to the homosexual ideal":

> Surely the faces of women are pleasant, but the taste of cheeks that have been newly shaved is better.

This "discovery" is attributed to a Turkish poet Jenab Shehabuddin. In his note E. P. M. writes "I have been able to find out no more about this very real poet than that he was born in 1870 and studied medicine and wrote much of his verse in Paris."

"He had a scholar's knowledge of French ... but he was not a good linguist", wrote E. Allen Ashwin. Mathers' sources for all the Eastern poems were collections in French translation. As, I think, a smokescreen for his own pseudonymous activities, he explains how he abandoned one already advertised part of *The Eastern Anthology* when he discovered that it was "a clever and entertaining French forgery". I think if assiduous search were made in those French collections he cites many other poems would be found to be by an E. P. M. alias. Especially those for which he provides notes.

His wife Rosamond observes sadly that his health prevented his fulfilment as an author. "A melancholy and self-distrustful temperament undermined his faith in his conceptions before they had attained full maturity" and "the pile of work brilliantly begun and laid aside mounted out of all proportion to that brought to completion." But many, especially the translations represented here, were also brilliantly completed. It seems that translation and pseudonyms were safer for his depressed and diffident talent, though he qualifies his invented Abu Nowas poems in *Red Wise* by saying, "I have not forgotten that my hero was a lyric poet of the first excellence. We must suppose that the examples ascribed to him were each written on an 'off day'."

The apologia and the pseudonymous gloss protect what is a sensitive real talent looking to the sensuality and sexual tenderness of the East for its poetic release. Rosamond also writes that the fame as Torquemada "in no way compensated for his disappointment as a creative artist." I feel that Mathers is placing himself with accustomed diffidence when he writes about the Chinese-American Julius Wing that "if I had had nothing to do with these poems ... I would say that Wing was a true poet, if only a true minor."

And Mathers, erotic aesthete, cocktail-shaking Chinese-American, honorary Arab nomad, *bhang*-chewer, Turkish bisexual, tormenting puzzle-setter, was a true if minor poet whose assimilation of Eastern modes should rank with Arthur Waley or Ezra Pound, and whose name and achievement should be much better known than they are. And the *Black Marigolds* of Edward Powys Mathers is a masterpiece that still affects me in the same way even now after almost fifty years. Perhaps even more with the "gala day" ever nearer. Even now!

TONY HARRISON
Newcastle-upon-Tyne, 2004

Coloured Stars

VERSIONS OF
FIFTY ASIATIC LOVE POEMS

to Rosamond Crowdy

THERE IS an opportunity of knowing in brilliant English translations much of the poetry of China and Japan, of India and Persia; and Arabic poetry is accessible; but I believe this book to be the first general English anthology of Asiatic verse. It is haphazard as such books must be until some polyglot scholar gives a whole life to the matter. Variety was the only aim possible in a space so small, and therefore I have selected love poems of different centuries and of both primitive and subtle peoples. If readers care to turn to *Anthologie de L'Amour Asiatique*, compiled by Adolphe Thalasso, the late editor of the *Revue Orientale* in Constantinople, they will find a full and clear study of Asia's love poetry and see also how much I owe to this erudite and stimulating authority. M. Thalasso's work first showed me beauty and interest in the songs of almost unknown literatures. In some instances I have translated directly and only from his book, in others I have gratefully taken his direction and traced poems back to their sources. Versions, also, of some of the Chinese poems given here will be found in the incomparable *Livre de Jade* of Mme. Judith Gautier. Reference to the texts of other poems is easily made at various libraries, except with regard to a dozen which I have personally collected. These last have not before, I think, been given a European form.

E. P. M.

London, 1918

Shade of the Orange Leaves

The young girl that in her chamber from dawn till eve alone
Broiders silk flowers on robes, deliciously shudders
At the unexpected sound of a far flute;
It seems to her that the voice of a young man is kissing her ear.

And when across the oiled paper
Of the high windows the orange leaves
Come and touch and make their shadows run on her knees
It seems to her that a hand is tearing her robe of silk.

From the Chinese of Tin-Tun-Ling

The Dalliance of the Leopards

Very afraid
I saw the dalliance of the leopards.
In the beauty of their coats
They sought each other and embraced.
Had I gone between them then
And pulled them asunder by their manes,
I would have run less risk
Than when I passed in my boat
And saw you standing on a dead tree
Ready to dive and kindle the river.

From the Sanskrit (5th Century)

War Song

To bodies straight as palm trees,
To hips as supple as reeds,
We prefer the straight staffs of our banners
Where suppl'ly floats our oriflamme of Sun,
Our banners gilt like cimitars
That catch the sunset.

To silk hair, red as burning coals,
To silk hair, black as coals burned out,
To hair that is dawn or night on girls' heads,
We prefer the tufts floating in fight,
Tufts of gold hair or of black hair
Pulled from the tails of our black horses.

To shining white breasts on virgin bodies,
Firm as the thrice tried bronze
And round like marble cups,
Whence subtle and swooning odours come,
We prefer the clash of our sabres triple tried
And the shining of our round shields like mighty cups.

To the murderous arrows of black eyes
Made blacker by the bow of brows
And the kohl of love given and love taken,
The dear darkness about eyes for love's sake,
We prefer the murderous arrows
That stretch our bows in fight.

The arrows of black eyes are tipped with kisses
Not kept back, not only sped at willing hearts,
And the tips gash chance hearts often enough
And give death where no battle is waged . . .
But the arrows of our bows
Sow death only among the hardy foe.

To bodies yielding under the struggle of love
And rearing under the red fire of kisses,
We prefer our horses tricked with silver and gold,
Our horses that yield not beneath us
And bound only at the sight of the blood of battles.

Altai

Black Hair

Last night my kisses drowned in the softness of black hair,
And my kisses like bees went plundering the softness of
    black hair.
Last night my hands were thrust in the mystery of black hair,
And my kisses like bees went plundering the sweetness of
    pomegranates
And among the scents of the harvest above my queen's neck,
    the harvest of black hair;
And my teeth played with the golden skin of her two ears.
Last night my kisses drowned in the softness of black hair,
And my kisses like bees went plundering the softness of
    black hair.

– Your kisses went plundering the scents of my harvest,
    O friend,
And the scents laid you drunk at my side. As sleep overcame
    Bahram
In the bed of Sarasya, so sleep overcame you on my bed.
I know one that has sworn your hurt for stealing the roses
    from my cheeks,
Has sworn your hurt even to death, the Guardian of black
    hair.
– Last night my kisses drowned in the softness of black hair,
And my kisses like bees went plundering the softness of
    black hair.

My hurt, darling? The sky will guard me if you wish me
   guarded.
But now for my defence, dearest, roll me a cudgel of black hair;
And give me the whiteness of your face, I am hungry for it
   like a little bird.
Still, if you wish me there, loosen me among the wantonness
   of black hair.
Last night my kisses drowned in the softness of black hair,
And my kisses like bees went plundering the softness of
   black hair.

Sweet friend, I will part the curtain of black hair and let you
   into the white garden of my breast.
But I fear you will despise me and not look back when you
   go away.
I am so beautiful and so white that the lamp-light faints to see
   my face,
And also God has given me for adornment my heavy black hair.
– Last night my kisses drowned in the softness of black hair,
And my kisses like bees went plundering the softness of
   black hair.

He has made you beautiful even among his most beautiful;
I am your little slave. O queen, cast me a little look.
I sent you the message of love at the dawn of day,
But my heart is stung by a snake, the snake of black hair.
Last night my kisses drowned in the softness of black hair,
And my kisses like bees went plundering the softness of
   black hair.

– Fear not, dear friend, I am the Charmer,
My breath will charm the snake upon your heart;
But who will charm the snake on my honour, my sad honour?
If you love me, let us go from Pakli. My husband is horrible.
From this forth I give you command over black hair.
– Last night my kisses drowned in the softness of black hair,
And my kisses like bees went plundering the softness of
    black hair.

Muhammadji has power over the poets of Pakli,
He takes tax from the Amirs of great Delhi.
He reigns over an empire and governs with a sceptre of
    black hair.
Last night my kisses drowned in the softness of black hair,
And my kisses like bees went plundering the softness of
    black hair.

From the Afghan of Muhammadji (19th Century)

The Garden of Bamboos

I live all alone, and I am a young girl.
I write long letters and do not know anyone to send them to.
Most tender things speak in my heart
And I can only say them to the bamboos in the garden.
Waiting on my feet, lifting the mat a little behind the door,
All day I watch the shadows of the people that pass.

A street song of Annam

Eyes That Move Not

The ashes are cold in the gold of the
    perfume-brazier. It is shaped like a
    fantastic lion.

Feverishly I fidget under the red wave
    of my bed-clothes, and suddenly I throw
    them from me to get up.

But I have not the courage to undertake
    my hair-dressing, the comb is too heavy
    for my dejection.

I leave the dust to tarnish the precious
    things on my toilet-table.

.   .   .   .

Already the sun has reached the height of
    the hasp that holds up the curtain.

This grief that I have hidden from all,
    this grief at a departure threatening,
    becomes more bitter still.

Things to say come as far as my lips,
    and I press them back into my heart.

It is indeed a new thing for me to feel
    a torment; this is not an illness caused
    by getting drunk, nor by the melancholy
    of approaching Autumn.

.   .   .   .

Ah, it is finished, it is finished.
He goes away to-day.

If I sang ten thousand times the
    "Stay here by me" song, yet he
    would not stay.

Now my mind has gone on a journey to the
    South; to his country, which is very far away.

Look, see, the mist encumbers my pavilion;
    before my eyes is but the water running round about.
    It is my grief's sole witness, and may be
    astonished to reflect so long and long the
    stupefaction of my eyes that move not.

Ah, heavier still, hereafter, shall my regard
    weigh down on you, pale mirror, for even as
    I speak it is accomplished, this harm,
    this sadness of eyes that move not.

From the Chinese of Ly-Y-Hane

Gazal

If the proud girl I love would cast a glance behind her,
As down the road she swings in her bright palanquin,
She would see her lover on foot, with empty hands.

Like the white buds of tuberose in a dark night
Through the lines of betel shine out her white teeth.

When she puts henna on her hands and dives in the soft river
One would think one saw fire twisting and running in the
    water.

From the Hindustani of Dilsoz (18th Century)

Doubt

Will he be true to me?
That I do not know.
But since the dawn
I have had as much disorder in my thoughts
As in my black hair.

From the Japanese of Hori-Kawa

Song

Like the fine and silky hair of our goats
Which climb up very high on the peaks
Of inaccessible Kara-Koroum,
So fine and silky is the hair of my girl.

Her eyes are soft as the eyes of the goats
That call their males on the mountain,
Her eyes are soft as the eyes of the goats
That hold the heavy teat to their young.

Her eyes have the colour of topaz
With which she decks her head and neck
And this topaz has the soft colour
Of the soft eyes, very soft eyes of our goats.

Her body apt for work is slight and supple,
As slight and supple as the bounds
Which our goats make, when they leap
On the curved flanks of the summit of Dapsang.

Her cheeks are ever fresh to my lips,
Fresh like the milk I draw daily
When the goats come back to the stable
From the swelling udders that sweep the ground.

Love song of Thibet

My Desire

When in your floating robe,
Woven with red silk and golden,
In your floating robe
Held round your hips
By a broidered belt,
Showing all curves
Of your reckless body,
You pass me by,
Eyeing me boldly
With provocative eyes,
And sending me from your lips
Teasing smiles,
Then I feel from your eyes,
Live like two diamonds
From the mines Sing Fos,
And from the smile of your lips
That smell so sweet of santal,
And from your breathing body
That your long robe shows,
I feel come to me
A wild and mad desire
Long, long to kiss your mouth
And your teeth painted with betel,
Long, long to possess
Your loving and breathing body,
Shown and hidden

By your long floating robe,
Woven with red silk and golden.
And this desire draws me to thee
As the oaks of Mandalay
Draw the lightning.

My desire is a stallion
That must have his mare,
My desire is a jaguar
Calling his female,
My desire is an elephant
Seeking his mate.
Your floating robe and your body,
Your eyes and your smile
Draw my desire to thee
As if your hands
Had passed chains
Through the rings of my ears
And dragged me
Even behind your feet,
As life draws breath
Desire draws me to thee.

When in the month of flowers
Snow piled on Youmadong
Falls from the mountain
In a devouring torrent,
Sweeps in his passage
Trees, houses, beasts and men,
And nothing is able

To stay his great course
That grows greater and greater
And drowns with his waters
The waters of Kin Douen;
So violent is my desire
For thy desire;
It overturns all things
In coming to thee,
It smothers the precepts
That Godama gave us,
And drowns all the laws
Of the Lord of the Elephant.

What does your husband matter?
What does your family matter?
I desire you, I long for you
With a wild and a mad love.
My desire is a torrent
Falling from the mountain,
Nothing can stay it.
It breaks and upheaves.
I desire you, I long for you
With a wild and a mad love.
I want to kiss your eyes,
I want to kiss your mouth,
I want to have
Your desire and your body;
No torrent is so strong
As my desire for your body.

The desire drawing me to thee
Is natural;
Like the torrent that falls
From the heights of Youmadong,
Like the lightning which falls
On the oaks of Mandalay,
Of nature natural
Is the desire that draws me to thee.

From the Burmese of Asmapour (19th Century)

Distich

Ah, would that I could hide within my songs
And, every time you sang them, kiss your lips.

From the Persian of Oumara (10th Century)

Song

Since you love me and I love you
The rest matters not;
I will cut grass in the fields
And you will sell it for beasts.

Since you love me and I love you
The rest matters not;
I will sow maize in the fields
And you will sell it for people.

Kafiristan

The Emperor

On a throne of new gold the Son of the Sky
    is sitting among his Mandarins. He shines
    with jewels and is like a sun surrounded by stars.

The Mandarins speak gravely of grave things;
    but the Emperor's thought has flown out by
    the open window.

In her pavilion of porcelain the Empress is
    sitting among her women. She is like a bright
    flower among leaves.

She dreams that her beloved stays too long
    at council, and wearily she moves her fan.

A breathing of perfumed air kisses the face
    of the Emperor.

"My beloved moves her fan, and sends me a
    perfume from her lips."

Towards the pavilion of porcelain walks the
    Emperor, shining with his jewels; and leaves his
    grave Mandarins to look at each other in silence.

From the Chinese of Thou-Fou

Song

You would climb after nectarines
In your little green jacket and puffy white drawers;
So that you fell and I caught you.
You made as if to break away,
And then settled wriggling in my arms,
All your lightness and softness were pressed against me,
And your face looked up from my breast
Puckered with amusement.
It would be something of the sort
If our clear blue night full of white stars
Turned to a night of coloured stars –
Red and purple and green to the zenith,
And orange and light violet and lemon,
And bright rose and crimson all about the sky.

From the Chinese (19th Century)

Love Song

The mountains of Bech-Parma are great enough,
But my love is greater.

The glaciers that marble their tops are white,
But your breasts are whiter.

The antelope stricken by my bullet
Weeps s a red blood from its wound

Which dyes with large red flowers
The field of the blowing jasmine flowers of snow.

Your arms are whiter than the jasmine flowers of snow;
And your kiss is redder than the blood of the antelope.

The mountains of Bech-Parma are great enough,
But my love is greater.

II

The wind screaming in the forest when the wind of Russia
    blows
Is milder than the desire that draws me to thee.

Your body smells richer than the resin
That weeps in the sun from slender pines.

And your mouth has more of odours
Than mint flowers throw on the air.

When you are by my side, I feel in my body
A warmth more suave than the softest sun-rays.

And when you go away from me, my sadness
Is blacker than the lowering night great with storm.

The wind screaming in the forest when the wind of Russia
    blows
Is milder than the desire that draws me to thee.

Daghestan

Fardiyat

I'd wish them to put for a talisman on my tomb a pink stone;
To remind folk of the stone heart and the pink fairness of
    my murderess.

From the Hindustani of Schah Selim (18th Century)

Loving Things

I am only a man, and yet sometimes
The green skin of unripened limes
Or the rose and gold of a naked heel
Take hold of my heart and make it feel.

And then I'm a god, that tints and blends,
Loves and laughs and comprehends;
Hunger and honour are my creed,
And the splendour of a windy speed.

And then I'm a wolf, that glares and runs
After the soft four-footed ones;
Moonlight is shattered on my track
Ere human voices call me back.

Modern Persian (author unknown)

Being Together at Night

By black water and dark blue water,
Making the wide tree balance its branches
Between us and the moon,
We stood close. As close among the leaves
Small green diamonds of rain
And the far stars.

From the Chinese (19th Century)

The Peach Flower

I have plucked from the branch of the peach a flower quite
    little, a flower quite rose;
And offered it to the loved girl whose lips are smaller and
    more rose than the little flower.

I have taken a swallow with black wings from its nest and
    offered it to the loved girl,
Whose lips are little and rose and whose brows are like the
    black wings of the swallow.

Next day the little rose flower was faded
And the swallow, following the soul of the flower, had taken
    flight
By the window open on to the Blue Mountain.

But on the lips of the loved girl flowers blow always small
    and rose,
And the black brows over her eyes have no air of wishing
    to beat their wings.

From the Chinese of Tse-Tie

Leila

Oh! Leila!
In your mouth are three things
A range of Bahrain pearls,
A goblet of Shiraz wine,
The musk of Thibet;
The musk of Thibet is your breath,
The Shiraz wine the water of your mouth,
The Bahrain pearls your teeth.
Oh! Leila!

Oh! Leila!
In your eyes are three things,
Black diamonds of Hindustan,
Figured silks of Lahore,
Flames of Fusi-Yama;
The mountain flames are their brightness,
The figured silks of Lahore their dusk,
The black diamonds of Hindustan their colour.
Oh! Leila!

Oh! Leila!
In your heart are three things,
All the yellow cobras of Burma,
All the deadly fungi of Bengal,
All Nepal's poison flowers;

The poison flowers are your vows,
The deadly fungi your kisses,
The yellow cobras your deceits.
Oh! Leila!

Song of Nepal

Looking at the Moon

Very far from your eyes
My loving eyes regard
The sky of stars.
Ah, that the moon might be
Changed to a mirror.

From the Japanese of a Courtezan of Nagasaki

Song

Dew on the bamboos,
Cooler than dew on the bamboos
Is putting my cheek against your breasts.

The pit of green and black snakes,
I would rather be in the pit of green and black snakes
Than be in love with you.

From the Sanskrit (5th Century)

A Love Rapture

Round the Palace of Waters gently the wind
    moves the flowers of the water-lilies.

On the highest terrace of Kou-Sou one sees
    the King of Lou lazily lying.

And before him Sy-Che, after whom beauty was
    named, dances with lovely grace of delicate
    weak gestures.

Then she laughs that she is so voluptuously
    weary, and languidly leans to the East on
    the white jade of the royal bed.

From the Chinese of Li-Tai-Pe

English Girl

I that lived ever about you
Never touched you, Lilian;
You came from far away
And devils with twitching faces
Had all their will of you
For gold.
But I saw your little feet in your bedroom,
Your little heathen shoes I kept so bright.
For they regarded not your feet, Lilian,
But I regarded.
Your little heathen stockings were mine to carry
And to set out and to wash.
They regarded not your feet,
But I that lived ever about you
Never touched you, Lilian.
Their faces twitch more this frosty morning;
They have put you in a heathen box
And hidden your feet and carried you out in the frosty morning.
They have passed with you over the foggy brook
And look like big blue men in the mist on the other side.
Now only the mist and the water remain.
They never regarded your feet,
But I regarded, Lilian.
Their faces ever twitched,
But, for the seven years since I saw you

My face did not change.
They never regarded your warm feet,
But I regarded.

From the Chinese (19th Century)

Gazal

Seeing me come the heavenly girl fled very fast,
And ran surpassing fast, her tongue between her teeth.
I followed, and the heavenly girl at the noise of my following
Pulled back the leaf of the door and hid behind.
I followed, and for her savagery fast, fast I scolded her;
Till all ashamed and drawing back she could not answer me . . .
Why starts the morning cock his chant so fast, so fast?
An evil cock, an evil chant to shatter my delight . . .
And this song is only as threads of smoke to the heavenly girl,
That vanish surpassing fast upon the winds of Spring.

From the Hindustani of Inscha (18th Century)

Lover's Jealousy

Although you are as beautiful as Kashmir at dawn
I am not jealous, O my wanton bird,
Of the lover that you have chosen, who takes my place
To-night upon your bed. You can ask me to your feasting
    to-night.
I carry the scent of your body about with me.

Fear not. I will bring things to eat and things to drink;
Since love makes the belly hungry and the throat dry.
And I'll sing my finest ballads, for which you used to pay
Your mendicant of love with diamonds of tears, pearls of
    laughter and rubies of kisses.
I carry the scent of your body about with me.

I will serve up to you all panting, all hot, and all crisp,
My heart which your spurns have made into roast lamb;
And for your thirst I will give you in a cup
In place of milk all the blood of my veins that you wish
    empty of my love.
I carry the scent of your body about with me.

I'll sing to your handsome the words you love, words that
    distilled in your ears
Make you all ripe to offer the cup of kisses,
Words I made for you yesterday, the beggar at your door,
Which to-day you want to hear cried by other lips.
I carry the scent of your body about with me.

I will sing him a ghazel of the learned way
To loose your hair and unravel your heavy black tresses,
Heavy with perfumes and little coins, with flowers and
    pearl-encrusted combs,
Heavy above all with the odour of your body.
I carry the scent of your body about with me.

Oh, this scent floating from your neck, your breasts,
    your arms;
That circles about your thighs and your little belly;
This scent that is fed for ever and for ever
From two shady flasks under your bright arms.
I carry the scent of your body about with me.

Oh, this hot scent that curdles my desire,
Odour of honey and santal, of milk and rose water,
And over all your little hot skin under great love
Breathing of amber.
I carry the scent of your body about with me.

I will sing him the very slow way
Of plucking date-sweet kisses from your lips,
Of plucking from your breasts all blowing flowers, carnations
    and roses,
And from between your breasts all fruits, oranges, peaches
    and strawberries.
I carry the scent of your body about with me.

And to place his head on your shoulder, O little bird,
Where, big and proud, your grain of beauty lies,

Like a black carnation in a desert of snow,
Like a black star in daylight.
I carry the scent of your body about with me.

My songs will teach him the things that made you mad,
What twistings you love, my serpent,
They'll murmur him what languors break your feline limbs,
And above all how to be loved by thee.
I carry the scent of your body about with me.

I want to light in his heart the flame that burns in me,
To see him suffer to-morrow, when you leave him for me,
All the torments that I have to-day.
You can ask *Rahchan* to your feasting to-night,
Rahchan will bring things to eat and things to drink . . .
I carry the scent of your body about with me.

From the Afghan of Mirza Rahchan Kayil

Spring Cold

In the melancholy enclosure

The wind leans, and drags at the threads of fine rain.

It is a good thing the double doors are shut.

The grace of the willows, the frailness of the
 flowers, these bow down before the capricious
 weather that rains towards the time of "Cold Feasts".

But whatever the weather, it is always difficult
 to find the balanced harmony of verse.

In the meanwhile; this much poetry is finished.

    .   .   .   .

What sweet thing may sustain, what sweet thing
 may console him who wakes from drunkenness? . . .
 the drunkenness of poetry, which is other than
 the drunkenness of wine? . . .

The wild swans have just passed.

Ah, I have a thousand sad things which I would
 confide to these rapid riders.

    .   .   .   .

In these days the Spring cold can be felt
in the upper storey.

On four sides the blinds are down in front
of the windows.

I am too dissatisfied to go and lean on
the jade balustrade.

The coverlet is cold, All the perfume is burned away.

I wake from my last dream.

Why are not people with great sorrows
forbidden to dream?

The colourless dew is falling into the water.

The trees are getting green again.

Quite a lot of people will rejoice to see
the Spring come back.

The sun is coming out, the mist is drifting away.

To-day I suppose I will have to look at some more
fine weather.

From the Chinese of Ly-Y-Hane

Climbing Up to You

I sang of a glass of crystal shadows lifting to mine
With shadows of rose lips upon the rim;
I sang of love kissed asleep by other girls
That after his rest would have as sweet a waking;
I sang of my life smashed like a hawk's egg
Against the granite stairs.
Now that I can climb
Pardon me two things –
That I gave not, round the beauty of your feet,
Bright coloured songs to moan for ever more,
That now, climbing, once or twice
Being weary I shade my mouth and sing
Of my heart's blood sweetened to a red grape
For you to bite and swallow and have done.

From the Arabic of John Duncan

Grief

If grief like fire should give out smoke
Ever it would be night on earth.

From the Persian of Schahid (10th Century)

Song

If you love God, take your mirror between your hands
    and look
How beautiful are your breasts with their two russet berries.
At sight of them, stricken, drunken, I cannot make a
    distinction
Between them and white roses beaten in white snow.
How beautiful are your breasts with their two russet berries.

No soul could be strong against your so bright eyes,
My desire hungers, for the kisses of one night did not fill it.
For love of God, take your mirror between your hands and
    judge
If a man could tire in looking on your face.
My desire hungers, for the kisses of one night did not fill it;
How beautiful are your breasts with their two russet berries.

From the Turkish of Mahmoud Djellaladine Pacha (19th Century)

Last Time

One more time
Before I quit the world
I want to see you,
To carry with me down there
Your face of love, O my love.

From the Japanese of Idzumi-Siki-Bu (10th Century)

Mokcha

(Supreme Happiness)

Like the bright drop
Which, from the perfumed womanhood
Of loving night,
Night amorous ever,
Tireless in her couplings
With the body of the world,
Falls in the virgin breast
Of a rose, and straightway
Ravishes her and shows

In its tiny globe
All the work of Brahma,
All the sky and all the earth;

So the drop of the dew
Of thy love, which trembles
On the petals of my heart,
Reflects in my love
The sky of the soul,
So sought Nirvana;

My love is Mokcha
Making me, from on earth,
Taste the high savour
Of immaterial joy.
Through thy love I have felt
That my essence is god-like
And that I am part
Of the world's Creator.

From the Burmese of Megdan (19th Century)

Gazal

When you have thrown torture and desire, O cruel child,
Into your lover's heart with lissom coquetries,
You sit down, calm and unmoved and never noticing,
And put desirous order into the loosened tangles of your hair.

And I watching you think of a placid pilgrim
That has come to camp and sits taking his ease,
With never a thought for his fellows on the road.
And I watching you think of the unconscious earth
Carelessly drinking the tears from wounded hearts.

From the Hindustani of Isch (18th Century)

Vai! Tchodjouklareum

Ah! my children! do you know Djemileh,
The turquoise, the carnation, the most beautiful girl in Bagdad?
Ah! my children!

Ah! my children! her face has aspects of the moon,
And in each of her eyes there is a sun.
Ah! my children!

Ah! my children! sometimes she leaves her vest unfastened,
Forgetting – who knows? – that it hides her breasts.
Ah! my children!

Ah! my children! she has round rosy paps
Standing straight out like peaches not yet ripe.
Ah! my children!

Ah! my children! look at the curve of her back;
She might crack nuts below her waist there.
Ah! my children!

Ah! my children! what shall be said of her thighs,
What so good to dream of as her thighs?
Ah! my children!

Ah! my children! Djemileh has just passed
Appetising and gilt like a cake for Ramazan.
Ah! my children!

Ah! my children! she comes down from the mountains
With her arms full of flowers, those little flowers that never die.
Ah! my children!

Ah! my children! the wind makes cling to her skin
Her rose robe, and makes her look quite naked.
Ah! my children!

Ah! my children! Djemileh comes to us to sell
The little flowers that never die, plucked in the mountain.
Ah! my children!

Ah! my children! when she sells her flowers
The bright eyes of the lads bathe her and devour her.
Ah! my children!

Ah! my children! eyes that pass through her robe
And do not count the money she gives back.
Ah! my children!

Ah! my children! feeling hands that tickle her
And she laughs with all her teeth, pulling back her veil.
Ah! my children!

Ah! my children! Djemileh has sold the flowers from the
       mountain;
And added to her dowry for marrying the hill boy she loves.
Ah! my children!

Kurdistan

The Mirror

I have saddled your raven horse with nervous limbs,
I have polished your sword, your rifle, and your lance.
Go, soldier, since you must; go, my eyes' joy:
But in your fights do not forget I love you.

As in the tiny mirror
Which you brought me from Kiachta Fair,
Promise that my face
Will be mirrored in your thought.

Before you go, make this promise –
To watch every evening at the third hour
The moon flashing in the sky
Like a great mirror of silver.

Before you go, I make this promise too –
To watch every evening at the third hour
The moon flashing in the sky
Like a great mirror of silver.

Thus every night, I'll seem to see your eyes,
Thus every night, you'll seem to see my eyes,
As in a silver mirror
In the moon, flashing in the sky.

Who knows but that perhaps the moon,
Moved to see our eyes hunting each other every night,
May consent really to change
Into a great mirror of silver.

Then I could watch you every night
Fighting on your raven horse;
And you could tell yourself every night
That I was keeping my promise.

Street Song of Eastern Mongolia

Fardiyat

The heartless girl, that was the cause of Saquib's death, saw
    his bier passing
And dared to ask of its sorrowful convoy the name of the man
    they were carrying to earth.

From the Hindustani of Saquib (18th Century)

At the East Gate

At the East Gate of the City are young women,
Gracious and light as clouds in Spring time;
But it does not move me that they have the lightness of clouds –
Under her thick veil and the whiteness of her robe, my love
   gives me all joy.

At the West Gate of the City are young women,
Sparkling and beautiful like the flowers of Spring time;
But it does not move me that they have the sparkling beauty
   of flowers –
Under her thick veil and the whiteness of her robe, my love
   gives me all joy.

From the Chinese Shi King (1776 BC)

Submission

When you have bathed in the river
On the moon's third day,
You make yourself, ah, so the more to be desired
By slipping on a robe the colour of your body.
Tell me, child, are three baskets of saffron enough
To colour your breasts and your arms and your face?

No other girl knows, like you, how to entice me,
Walking alone in the shadows of the palm trees.
None has your tickling gestures, your enflaming eyes –
So young, so smooth, and so flower fresh,
You must have more men silly about you
Than there are corners in your bedroom to hide them.

In the morning when I come to see you under the verandah
Just for the pleasure of talking to you;
Or in the evening when I curry favour with the poulterer
Just for the pleasure of feeling myself near you;
Or at night when my hand seeks to clasp you
Through the hole pierced in the planking by your bed;
Your mother can say all she likes,
Reproaches, insults, swear-words. I accept all in advance.
But I conjure you do not refuse me
A quite small corner of your bedroom in which to hide.

From the Siamese

In the Palace

What rigorous calm! What almost holy silence!
    All the doors are shut, and the beds of flowers
    are giving out scent; discreetly of course . . .

Two women that lean against each other, stand to
    the balustrade of red marble on the edge of the
    terrace.

One of them wishes to speak, to confide to her
    friend the secret sorrow that is agonizing her heart.

She throws an anxious glance at the motionless leaves,
    and because of a paroquet with iridescent wings
    that perches on a branch, she sighs and is silent.

From the Chinese of Thou-Sin-Yu

A Thing Remembered

I'll not forget the warm blue night when my bold girl,
Whose kissing lips smell sweet of honey and rose water,

Came softly to my room, and my room glowed
As if the moon at her bright full had entered to me.

"Press me in your arms," she said. "All that your love demands
Ask and obtain. My old watching woman is far away."

I pressed her in my arms, and said: "Your robe is a curtain.
Wherefore a curtain between me and thee, violet joy of my
heart?"

And so saying, I began to undo some parts of her robe.
She looked smiling at me and I, also smiling, unloosed and
unloosed.

"My joy, the flower in her bud pleases me not:
And fruit hanging under leaves delights me not.

"My sword I love not in its sheath, it is no pleasure
To see the stars of night hidden behind clouds."

From the Arabic

The Most Virtuous Woman

Pluck the most beautiful apricot from this tree
And place it on silk in a coffer of sandal-wood;
At the end of three days the silk
Will be stained by the juice of the fruit.

Choose the most virtuous woman from this world,
Place her image in the coffer of your heart,
Even on the same instant your heart
Will be soiled with bad thoughts.

Popular Song of Manchuria

The Meeting

A summer's night I met my girl on the path
That leads straight to her dwelling and straight to my tent.

We were alone, we two, without watchers or informers,
Far from the tribe, far from jealous eyes and spying ears
    and harming tongues.

I laid my face on the ground, my brow a footstool for my girl.
She said: "Open your heart with joy, we are without watchers;
Come press your lips to my veil."

But my lips would not consent to it.
I felt that I had two honours to guard,
My girl's and mine.

And, as was my desire, we were all night together,
Near to each other, far from the tribe and spying eyes.

And it seemed that I was master
Of all the kingdoms of the world, and that the elements
Obeyed me as slaves.

From the Arabic of Ibn-el-Fared (1220 AD)

The Drunken Rose

Has not the night been as a drunken rose
Without a witness? And the girl of bloom
Has given up all. What little cries of joy!
What wanton words repeated!
But white dawn shows the rose and green pet bird,
The mighty talker and awake all night.
Hark! The old woman comes; he will tell all.
What shall she, fluttering? Snap small rubies off
From the bright ear-rings, facets sharp as steel:
These with the seed-pulp of the passion-fruit,
His sweet prepared breakfast, mingle featly . . .
So, busy jargoner, silent for ever more.

From the Sanskrit of Amorou (1st Century)

The Tryst

In thy presence my arms, my hands, my lips, all my being,
Tremble as tremble the leaves
Of the cinnamon-apples shaken by the wind.

– The leaves of the cinnamon-apple do not tremble, O my love.
They shiver under the caress of the wind
Which drinks deep of their perfumed kisses.

Come with me to-night under the cinnamon-apples
And like their leaves you will shiver under my caress,
And like the wind I will drink deep of your perfumed kisses.

I will come. But what will you give me for my kisses?
– For your kisses I offer you my kisses.
What will you give me for my heart?
– For your heart I offer you my heart.
What will you give me for my love?
– For your love I offer you my life.

I accept your kisses and your heart and your life;
And I give in exchange myself to be all yours.
And all trembling this night I will come to offer you my kisses
Under the cinnamon-apples caressed by the wind
And in the wind that drinks deep of their perfumed kisses.

By an unknown author of Camboja

Zulma

I seemed to see behind a half-opened door
Two roses on a rose-tree.
I was mistaken.
It was not really two roses
But the curved cheeks of Zulma.

I seemed to see behind a half-opened door
Two white lily flowers.
I was mistaken.
It was not really two white lily flowers
But the curved breasts of Zulma.

I seemed to see behind a half-opened door
Two red blossoms of the passion-flower,
I was mistaken.
It was not really two red blossoms of the passion-flower
But the curved lips of Zulma.

Women or flowers, what matter? Tell the girl
That my gardens are great and great my women's quarters.
There grow the red and the rose and the white flowers,
And the light women and the dark women, with skins of
    amber and ivory,
And that I wish to pluck the rose flowers of her cheeks
And the red flowers of her lips and the white flowers of
    her breasts.

Street Song of Baluchistan

Rubaiyat

They've assured me that Paradise is full of girls,
They've assured me that I'll find wine and honey in Paradise.
Well then, why forbid me wine and girls down here,
Seeing that up there my reward will be girls and wine?

From the Persian of Omar Khayam (10th Century)

Picture

I see the snowy winter sky through the old arch;
And in the middle the line of one tree.
A flight of crows comes just above the tree,
Sweeping to left and right, and tailing out behind.
I think of you.

From the Japanese (18th Century)

White

I thought that it was snowing
Flowers. But, no. It was this young lady
Coming towards me.

From the Japanese of Yori-Kito (19th Century)

Song

I came upon you rolling in the grass,
Like a young beast you rolled over and over,
Flinging your legs wide,
Flinging your arms wide,
And rubbing against the dew.
I came upon you rolling in the grass
And crept away.

From the Sanskrit (5th Century)

The Red Lotus

A flower opens down under the deep water . . .
    the deep water.

I take a cord and throw it towards the flower
    whose roots are so far down.

Whose roots are so far down.

The mystery of the deep darkness is troubled,
    the repose ceases, the ripple spreads very far.

With my cord I try to snare the lotus; as if his
    heart were deep there in the water.

The sun floats on the extreme edge of the sky,
    he goes down, he goes out, he falls into the night
    and drowns.

He falls into the night and drowns.

   .   .   .   .

I climb up again to the highest storey; I stop
    in front of my mirror; a tragic and wasted face!

A tragic and wasted face!

The plants are setting about to become green again,
and to put out new shoots.

How have I managed, without hope, to reach this day?

From the Chinese of Ly-Y-Hane

Envoy

The night before last night
I heard that to make songs to girls
And to make prayers to God
Were of equal value
In the eyes of time;
Provided, that is,
That the prayers
Are sufficiently beautiful.

From the Burmese

FOUR NOTES

Black Hair (p. 25)

For many of the forty years of his life, which closed in madness in 1890, Muhammadji, the greatest poet of Afghanistan, was working out sentences in prison for violent brawling and heavy drinking. In the last stanza of this poem the folly of grandeurs is easily detected; and in all his work, mingled with that drowsy music which was his greatness, is a vertigo from over the depths of insanity.

English Girl (p. 50)

This poem, which could only have been thought in a Chinese brain, is yet in form very wide of modern Chinese tradition. Its author, who also wrote *Song* (p. 29) and *Being Together at Night* (p. 34), is an American born Chinese, a valet by profession, and by instinct an artist both in words and colours.

Lover's Jealousy (p. 52)

Mirza (Prince) Rahchan Kayil was the pen-name of Hussein Izzat Rafi, a popular contemporary of Muhammadji. Being a fine linguist and tireless traveller, he explored the wildest parts of Asia and the most ordinary capitals of Europe, searching out inspiration for a mystical work which should reconcile all religions. At the age of 48 he was hanged for supposed complicity in a plot against the Shah of Persia.

Climbing Up to You (p. 57)

John Duncan died in his middle age this year, and left only the short-lived memory of a brilliant talker and a few strange poems in the language of his adoption. How far he had identified his being with the Arabs, among whom he lived and had married, may be gathered from his serious use of the expression "A tourist, pure and simple," when speaking of the late Sir Richard Burton. This poem is the only one of his which seemed to be generally comprehensible without those verbal annotations which it was his custom sometimes to supply when reading.

Black Marigolds

To My Wife

*And sometimes we look to the end of the tale
that there should be marriage-feasts, and find
only, as it were, black marigolds and a silence.*

– AZEDDIN EL MOCADECCI

NINETEEN hundred years ago, when Bhartrihari was writing, Chauras, a young Brahman poet, lived at the Court of King Sundava in Kanchinpur, and loved Vidya, the king's daughter. It is said that on the discovery of their love Chauras was imprisoned and executed; and that it was in the last few hours of his life that he composed his love lament, the *Chaurapanchasika*: "the Fifty Stanzas of Chauras."

Though the poem which is printed here has verses of direct, almost literal, translation, it would be fairer to Chauras to consider it, in its entirety, as an interpretation rather than as a translation of his work; an attempt to bring over into an English poem the spirit of mournful exaltation which informs his Sanskrit leave-taking.

I have tried to imitate the abrupt rise from earth which his poem makes about the fifteenth stanza; and I have also tried, by not letting my verse become a coherent lyric poem in the English sense, to keep his disjointed air, as of a set-form sequence, in which the stanzas are bound together only by a thread of feeling. Asia knows nothing, of the long lyric, save in that sense which could describe Rossetti's "House of Life" or Shakespeare's Sonnets.

The first "shloke" of each stanza in the original starts with *adyapi*, a word of reminiscence, and this gives to the poem a recurring monotone of retrospection, which I hope my unchanging *Even now* also suggests.

My rendering was finished in 1915, in two or three sessions on a box by the stove in hutments; and I have not cared to risk a discrepancy of moods in more luxurious minutes and places.

"Black Marigolds" is an isolated experiment, which tries to reinvigorate a few very old leaves of sad writing; and of its nature it stands apart from the Asiatic street songs and love songs which I have translated in "Coloured Stars", which has been published; and in the less tentative "Garden of Bright Waters", which Mr Blackwell will publish in the Spring.

E. P. M.

Lincoln's Inn Fields, 1919

EVEN NOW

My thought is all of this gold-tinted king's daughter
With garlands tissue and golden buds,
Smoke tangles of her hair, and sleeping or waking
Feet trembling in love, full of pale languor;
My thought is clinging as to a lost learning
Slipped down out of the minds of men,
Labouring to bring her back into my soul.

Even now
If I see in my soul the citron-breasted fair one
Still gold-tinted, her face like our night stars,
Drawing unto her; her body beaten about with flame,
Wounded by the flaring spear of love,
My first of all by reason of her fresh years,
Then is my heart buried alive in snow.

Even now
If my girl with lotus eyes came to me again
Weary with the dear weight of young love,
Again I would give her to these starved twins of arms
And from her mouth drink down the heavy wine,
As a reeling pirate bee in fluttered ease
Steals up the honey from the nenuphar.

[1–3]

Even now
I bring her back, ah, wearied out with love
So that her slim feet could not bear her up;
Curved falls of her hair down on her white cheeks;
In the confusion of her coloured vests
Speaking that guarded giving up, and her scented arms
Lay like cool bindweed over against my neck.

Even now
I bring her back to me in her quick shame,
Hiding her bright face at the point of day:
Making her grave eyes move in watered stars,
For love's great sleeplessness wandering all night,
Seeming to sail gently, as that pink bird,
Down the water of love in a harvest of lotus.

Even now
If I saw her lying all wide eyes
And with collyrium the indent of her cheek
Lengthened to the bright ear and her pale side
So suffering the fever of my distance,
Then would my love for her be ropes of flowers, and night
A black-haired lover on the breasts of day.

[4–6]

Even now
I see the heavy startled hair of this reed-flute player
Who curved her poppy lips to love dances,
Having a youth's face madding like the moon
Lying at her full; limbs ever moving a little in love,
Too slight, too delicate, tired with the small burden
Of bearing love ever on white feet.

Even now
She is present to me on her beds,
Balmed with the exhalation of a flattering musk,
Rich with the curdy essence of santal;
Girl with eyes dazing as the seeded wine,
Showing as a pair of gentle nut-hatches
Kissing each other with their bills, each hidden
By turns within a little grasping mouth.

Even now
She swims back in the crowning hour of love
All red with wine her lips have given to drink,
Soft round the mouth with camphor and faint blue
Tinted upon the lips, her slight body,
Her great live eyes, the colourings of herself
A clear perfection; sighs of musk outstealing
And powdered wood spice heavy of Cashmir.

[7–9]

Even now
I see her; far face blond like gold
Rich with small lights, and tinted shadows surprised
Over and over all of her; with glittering eyes
All bright for love but very love weary,
As it were the conjuring disk of the moon when Rahou ceases
With his dark stumbling block to hide her rays.

Even now
She is art-magically present to my soul,
And that one word of strange heart's ease, goodbye,
That in the night, in loth moving to go,
And bending over to a golden mouth,
I said softly to the turned away
Tenderly tired hair of this king's daughter.

Even now
My eyes that hurry to see no more are painting, painting
Faces of my lost girl. O golden rings
That tap against cheeks of small magnolia leaves,
O whitest so soft parchment where
My poor divorcèd lips have written excellent
Stanzas of kisses, and will write no more.

[10–12]

Even now
Death sends me the flickering of powdery lids
Over wild eyes and the pity of her slim body
All broken up with the weariness of joy;
The little red flowers of her breasts to be my comfort
Moving above scarves, and for my sorrow
Wet crimson lips that once I marked as mine.

Even now
By a cool noise of waters in the spring
The Asoka with young flowers that feign her fingers
And bud in red; and in the green vest pearls kissing
As it were rose leaves in the gardens of God; the shining
     at night
Of white cheeks in the dark; smiles from light thoughts
     within,
And her walking as of a swan: these trouble me.

Even now
The pleasèd intimacy of rough love
Upon the patient glory of her form
Racks me with memory; and her bright dress
As it were yellow flame, which the white hand
Shamefastly gathers in her rising haste,
The slender grace of her departing feet.

[13–15]

Even now
When all my heavy heart is broken up
I seem to see my prison walls breaking
And then a light, and in that light a girl
Her fingers busied about her hair, her cool white arms
Faint rosy at the elbows, raised in the sunlight,
And temperate eyes that wander far away.

Even now
I seem to see my prison walls come close,
Built up of darkness, and against that darkness
A girl no taller than my breast and very tired,
Leaning upon the bed and smiling, feeding
A little bird and lying slender as ash trees,
Sleepily aware as I told of the green
Grapes and the small bright coloured river flowers.

Even now
I see her, as I used, in her white palace
Under black torches throwing cool red light,
Woven with many flowers and tearing the dark.
I see her rising, showing all her face
Defiant timidly, saying clearly:
Now I shall go to sleep, good-night, my ladies.

[16–18]

Even now
Though I am so far separate, a flight of birds
Swinging from side to side over the valley trees,
Passing my prison with their calling and crying,
Bring me to see my girl. For very bird-like
Is her song singing, and the state of a swan
In her light walking, like the shaken wings
Of a black eagle falls her nightly hair.

Even now
I know my princess was happy. I see her stand
Touching her breasts with all her flower-soft fingers,
Looking askance at me with smiling eyes.
There is a god that arms him with a flower
And she was stricken deep. Here, oh die here.
Kiss me and I shall be purer than quick rivers.

Even now
They chatter her weakness through the two bazaars
Who was so strong to love me. And small men
That buy and sell for silver being slaves
Crinkle the fat about their eyes; and yet
No Prince of the Cities of the Sea has taken her,
Leading to his grim bed. Little lonely one,
You clung to me as a garment clings; my girl.

[19–21]

Even now
Only one dawn shall rise for me. The stars
Revolve to-morrow's night and I not heed.
One brief cold watch beside an empty heart
And that is all. This night she rests not well;
Oh, sleep; for there is heaviness for all the world
Except for the death-lighted heart of me.

Even now
My sole concern the slipping of her vests,
Her little breasts the life beyond this life.
One night of disarray in her green hems,
Her golden cloths, outweighs the order of earth,
Making of none effect the tides of the sea.
I have seen her enter the temple meekly and there seem
The flag of flowers that veils the very god.

Even now
I mind the coming and talking of wise men from towers
Where they had thought away their youth. And I, listening,
Found not the salt of the whispers of my girl,
Murmur of confused colours, as we lay near sleep;
Little wise words and little witty words,
Wanton as water, honied with eagerness.

[22–24]

Even now
I call to mind her weariness in the morning
Close lying in my arms, and tiredly smiling
At my disjointed prayer for her small sake.
Now in my morning the weariness of death
Sends me to sleep. Had I made coffins
I might have lived singing to three score.

Even now
The woodcutter and the fishermen turn home,
With on his axe the moon and in his dripping net
Caught yellow moonlight. The purple flame of fires
Calls them to love and sleep. From the hot town
The maker of scant songs for bread wanders
To lie under the clematis with his girl.
The moon shines on her breasts, and I must die.

Even now
I have a need to make up prayers, to speak
My last consideration of the world
To the great thirteen gods, to make my balance
Ere the soul journeys on. I kneel and say:
Father of Light. Leave we it burning still
That I may look at you. *Mother of the Stars,*
Give me your feet to kiss; I love you, dear.

[25–27]

Even now
I seem to see the face of my lost girl
With frightened eyes, like a wood wanderer,
In travail with sorrowful waters, unwept tears
Labouring to be born and fall; when white face turned
And little ears caught at the far murmur,
The pleased snarling of the tumult of dogs
When I was hurried away down the white road.

Even now
When slow rose-yellow moons looked out at night
To guard the sheaves of harvest and mark down
The peach's fall, how calm she was and love worthy.
Glass-coloured starlight falling as thin as dew
Was wont to find us at the spirit's starving time
Slow straying in the orchard paths with love.

Even now
Love is a god and Rati the dark his bride;
But once I found their child and she was fairer,
That could so shine. And we were each to each
Wonderful and a presence not yet felt
In any dream. I knew the sunset earth
But as a red gold ring to bear my emerald
Within the little summer of my youth.

[28–30]

Even now
I marvel at the bravery of love.
She, whose two feet might be held in one hand
And all her body on a shield of the guards,
Lashed like a gold panther taken in a pit
Tearfully valiant, when I too was taken;
Bearding her black beard father in his wrath,
Striking the soldiers with white impotent hands.

Even now
I mind that I loved cypress and roses, dear,
The great blue mountains and the small grey hills,
The sounding of the sea. Upon a day
I saw strange eyes and hands like butterflies;
For me at morning larks flew from the thyme
And children came to bathe in little streams.

Even now
Sleep left me all these nights for your white bed
And I am sure you sistered lay with sleep
After much weeping. Piteous little love,
Death is in the garden, time runs down,
The year that simple and unexalted ran till now
Ferments in winy autumn, and I must die.

[31–33]

Even now
I mind our going, full of bewilderment
As who should walk from sleep into great light,
Along the running of the winter river,
A dying sun on the cool hurrying tide
No more by green rushes delayed in dalliance,
With a clear purpose in his flower flecked length
Informed, to reach Nirvana and the sea.

Even now
I love long black eyes that caress like silk,
Ever and ever sad and laughing eyes,
Whose lids make such sweet shadow when they close
It seems another beautiful look of hers.
I love a fresh mouth, ah, a scented mouth,
And curving hair, subtle as a smoke,
And light fingers, and laughter of green gems.

Even now
I mind asking: Where love and how love Rati's priestesses?
You can tell me of their washings at moon down
And if that warm basin have silver borders.
Is it so that when they comb their hair
Their fingers, being purple stained, show
Like coral branches in the black sea of their hair?

[34–36]

Even now
I remember that you made answer very softly,
We being one soul, your hand on my hair,
The burning memory rounding your near lips:
I have seen the priestesses of Rati make love at moon fall
And then in a carpeted hall with a bright gold lamp
Lie down carelessly anywhere to sleep.

Even now
I have no surety that she is not Mahadevi
Rose red of Siva, or Kapagata
The wilful ripe Companion of the King,
Or Krisna's own Lakshmi, the violet haired.
I am not certain but that dark Brahma
In his high secret purposes
Has sent my soft girl down to make the three worlds mad
With capering about her scented feet.

Even now
Call not the master painters from all the world,
Their thin black boards, their rose and green and grey,
Their ashes of lapis lazuli ultramarine,
Their earth of shadows the umber. Laughing at art
Sunlight upon the body of my bride,
For painting not nor any eyes for ever.
Oh warm tears on the body of my bride.

[37–39]

Even now
I mind when the red crowds were passed and it was raining
How glad those two that shared the rain with me;
For they talked happily with rich young voices
And at the storm's increase, closer and with content,
Each to the body of the other held
As there were no more severance for ever.

Even now
The stainless fair appearance of the moon
Rolls her gold beauty over an autumn sky
And the stiff anchorite forgets to pray;
How much the sooner I, if her wild mouth
Tasting of the taste of manna came to mine
And kept my soul at balance above a kiss.

Even now
Her mouth carelessly scented as with lotus dust
Is water of love to the great heat of love,
A tirtha very holy, a lover's lake
Utterly sacred. Might I go down to it
But one time more, then should I find a way
To hold my lake for ever and ever more
Sobbing out my life beside the waters.

[40–42]

Even now
I mind that the time of the falling of blossoms started my
    dream
Into a wild life, into my girl;
Then was the essence of her beauty spilled
Down on my days so that it fades not,
Fails not, subtle and fresh, in perfuming
That day, and the days, and this the latest day.

Even now
She with young limbs as smooth as flower pollen,
Whose swaying body is laved in the cool
Waters of languor, this dear bright-coloured bird,
Walks not, changes not, advances not
Her weary station by the black lake
Of Gone Forever, in whose fountain vase
Balance the water-lilies of my thought.

Even now
Spread we our nets beyond the farthest rims
So surely that they take the feet of dawn
Before you wake and after you are sleeping
Catch up the visible and invisible stars
And web the ports the strongest dreamer dreamed,
Yet is it all one, Vidya, yet is it nothing.

[43–45]

Even now
The night is full of silver straws of rain,
And I will send my soul to see your body
This last poor time. I stand beside your bed;
Your shadowed head lies leaving a bright space
Upon the pillow empty, your sorrowful arm
Holds from your side and clasps not anything.
There is no covering upon you.

Even now
I think your feet seek mine to comfort them.
There is some dream about you even now
Which I'll not hear at waking. Weep not at dawn,
Though day brings wearily your daily loss
And all the light is hateful. Now is it time
To bring my soul away.

Even now
I mind that I went round with men and women,
And underneath their brows, deep in their eyes,
I saw their souls, which go slipping aside
In swarms before the pleasure of my mind;
The world was like a flight of birds, shadow or flame
Which I saw pass above the engraven hills.
Yet was there never one like to my girl.

[46–48]

Even now
Death I take up as consolation.
Nay, were I free as the condor with his wings
Or old kings throned on violet ivory,
Night would not come without beds of green floss
And never a bed without my bright darling.
It is most fit that you strike now, black guards,
And let this fountain out before the dawn.

Even now
I know that I have savoured the hot taste of life
Lifting green cups and gold at the great feast.
Just for a small and a forgotten time
I have had full in my eyes from off my girl
The whitest pouring of eternal light.
The heavy knife. As to a gala day.

[49–50]

Works by E. Powys Mathers

THIS LIST of works published during the author's lifetime was given in *Torquemada: 112 Best Crossword Puzzles*, edited by J. M. Campbell (Pushkin Press, London, 1942). The book is prefaced by Lord Dunsany's poem 'In Memory of a Great Translator' and memoirs of Mathers by Rosamond Mathers, John Dickson Carr and E. Allen Ashwin.

1919   *Coloured Stars*. Versions of Fifty Asiatic Love Poems. (Blackwell).
        Black Marigolds, being a rendering into English of the Panchasika of Chauras. (Blackwell).

1920   *The Garden of Bright Waters*. Versions of 120 Asiatic Love Poems. (Blackwell).

1923–4 *The Thousand Nights and One Night*, rendered from literal and complete version of Dr. J. C. Mardrus, collated with other sources. (The Casanova Society). A new and revised edition of this was published in 1937. (Routledge).

1924   *The Queen of Sheba*, from the French translation of his own Arabic text by Dr. J. C. Mardrus. (Casanova Society).

1925   *Sung to Shahryar*. Poems selected from the book of *The Thousand Nights and One Night*. (Casanova Society).

1926   *Crosswords for Riper Years*, by 'Torquemada'. A Series of Twelve Crosswords in Rhyme. (Routledge).
        The Procreant Hymn. (Golden Cockerel Press).
        Red Wise. (Golden Cockerel Press).

1926–8 *Eastern Love*. An Anthology of Oriental Tales and Verse. Published in England in two editions, of four and of twelve volumes, and in America (Liveright) in three volumes. (John Rodker).

1929   *A Circle of the Seasons*, a translation of the Ritu Samhara of Kalidasa, made from various European sources. (Golden Cockerel Press).

The Maxims of Chamfort. (Golden Cockerel Press).

1930   *Salammbo*, translated from the French of Gustave Flaubert. (Golden Cockerel Press).

1932   *The Amores of Ovid*. (Golden Cockerel Press).

1933   *Cold Blood*. A Detective-mystery play produced at the Duke of York's Theatre, London.

Love Night, a Gallantry, a play in prose and verse intended for a musical setting. (Published 1935, Golden Cockerel Press).

1934   *The Torquemada Puzzle Book*. (Gollancz).

1938   *Mademoiselle De Maupin*, translated from the French of Théophile Gautier. (Golden Cockerel Press).

Poetica

A series of texts, translations and miscellaneous works
relating to poetry

Some Asian and Oriental poetry in translation

FROM MODERN BENGALI

RABINDRANATH TAGORE: *Song Offerings*
(Gitanjali)
Translated by Joe Winter

JIBANANANDA DAS: *Naked Lonely Hand*
Selected Poems
Translated by Joe Winter

FROM CLASSICAL CHINESE

LI HE: *Goddesses, Ghosts, and Demons*
Translated by J. D. Frodsham

LI PO: *The Selected Poems of Li Po*
Translated by David Hinton

PO CHÜ-I: *The Selected Poems of Po Chü-i*
Translated by David Hinton

TU FU: *The Selected Poems of Tu Fu*
Translated by David Hinton

FROM KOREAN CHINESE

Slow Chrysanthemums
Classical Korean Poems in Chinese
Translated by Kim Jong-gil

FROM CONTEMPORARY CHINESE

BEI DAO: *The August Sleepwalker*
Translated by Bonnie S. McDougall

BEI DAO: *Old Snow*
Translated by Bonnie S. McDougall and Chen Maiping

BEI DAO: *Forms of Distance*
Translated by David Hinton

BEI DAO: *Landscape Over Zero*
Translated by David Hinton with Yanbing Chen

BEI DAO: *Unlock*
Translated by Eliot Weinberger & Iona Man-Cheong